Ways to....

WEAR *it!*

Henry Pluckrose

Photography by Chris Fairclough

FRANKLIN WATTS

London • New York • Sydney • Toronto

Have you thought about the things you are wearing today?

There are many
kinds of clothes.

**People wear
different clothes
at different times.**

Whatever you are wearing, it's important that it fits.

Clothes are made to fit the tall and the small, the young and the old.

People wear
different clothes
around the world.

Why do you think the people are wearing different kinds of clothes?

What are you wearing on your feet? Boots or shoes, trainers or slippers, lace-ups or slip-ons?

Whatever you are wearing, it's important that they feel comfortable.

Hats can be fun to wear!

What other reasons are there for wearing a hat?

Some people wear uniforms to work. Why is it important that they are easily recognized?

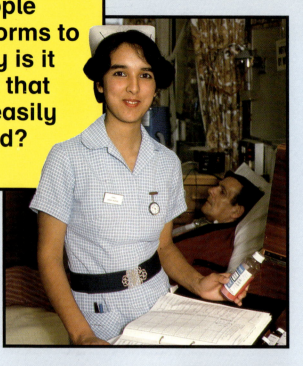

Some people wear special clothes to protect themselves. Why do these people need to wear protective clothing?

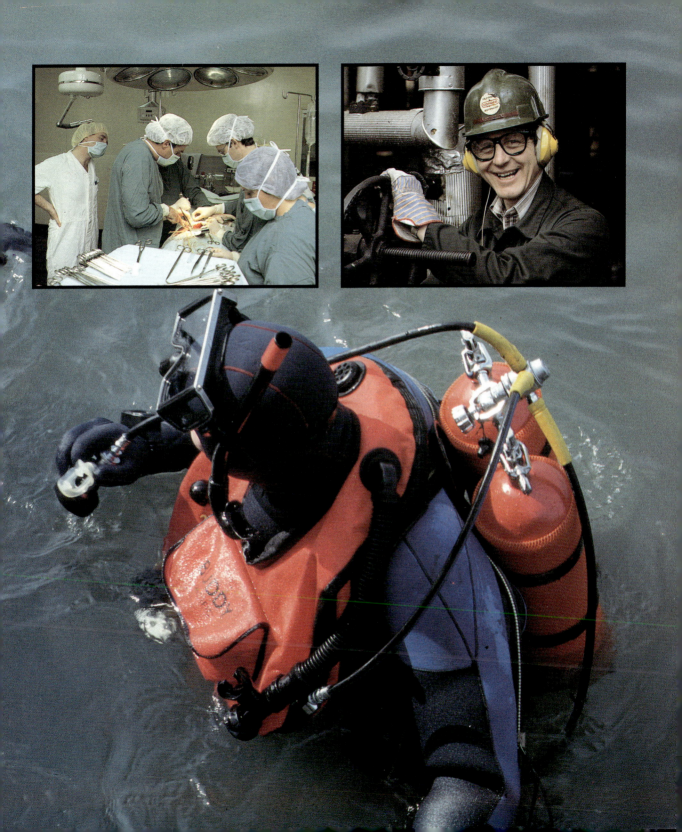

People who play sports need special clothes too.

They wear them for protection ... to move more easily ... or to show what team they are in.

People dress up for special occasions ... carnivals, weddings, parades, dancing in the streets ...

When did you last dress up?

Can you tell what these people are doing from what they are wearing?

Some things for you to do

● Find pictures of different kinds of clothes in old magazines and newspapers. Cut the pictures out and stick them in a scrap book. Put all the hats together on one page, the coats on another ... and so for all types of clothes.

● How many different sorts of hats can you and your friends collect? Make a little display of them. Can you find some hard hats and some soft ones?

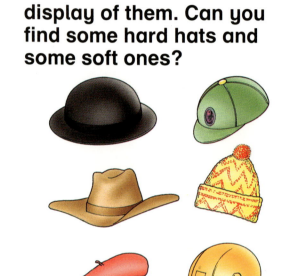

● Think of the many ways to get your clothes clean. Which clothes can we clean at home? Which clothes do we have to take to a special shop?

● Look in your clothes drawer. What clothes do you only wear in the winter? What clothes do you only wear in the summer? What clothes do you wear all the year around? Why are some warmer than others?

● Make a scrapbook collection of pictures of people in clothes from different parts of the world.

● Find a piece of material and make yourself a hat. You could decorate it with a feather or ribbon.

● Look at the labels on the inside of your clothes. These labels usually tell you how the clothes should be cleaned. Ask an adult to explain the symbols to you.

● How many things are you wearing which are not clothes?

Words about wearing

anorak	jumper	shirt	drape	casual	smart
blazer	kaftan	shorts	fasten	comfortable	stretchy
blouse	kagoul	skirt	dress	cool	tailored
coat	kimono	socks	dress up	fashionable	tight
dress	kilt	sweatshirt	put on	fitted	warm
dungarees	leggings	T-shirt	take off	formal	
gloves	mac	tights	tie	informal	
jacket	pants	trousers	undo	itchy	
jeans	pinafore	underwear	wrap up	loose	
jersey	sari	uniform	zip	scruffy	
jodhpurs	sarong	vest		sloppy